PICTUREPEDIA

NOTE TO PARENTS

This book is part of PICTUREPEDIA, a completely
new kind of information series for children.
Its unique combination of pictures and words
encourages children to use their eyes to discover and
explore the world, while introducing them to a wealth
of basic knowledge. Clear, straightforward text
explains each picture thoroughly and provides
additional information about the topic.

"Looking it up" becomes an easy task with
PICTUREPEDIA, an ideal first reference for all types of
schoolwork. Because PICTUREPEDIA is also entertaining,
children will enjoy reading its words and looking
at its pictures over and over again. You can encourage
and stimulate further inquiry by helping your child
pose simple questions for the whole family to
"look up" and answer together.

MACHINES

A DK PUBLISHING BOOK

Consultant John Farndon
Editor Hilary Hockman
Designers Flora Awolaja, Sarah Goodwin,
Tuong Nguyen, Samantha Webb
U.S. Editor B. Alison Weir
Series Editor Sarah Phillips
Series Art Editor Paul Wilkinson
Picture Researcher Miriam Sharland
Production Manager Ian Paton
Production Assistant Harriet Maxwell
Editorial Director Jonathan Reed
Design Director Ed Day

First American edition, 1993
4 6 8 10 9 7 5

Published in the United States by
DK Publishing, Inc., 95 Madison Avenue
New York, New York 10016

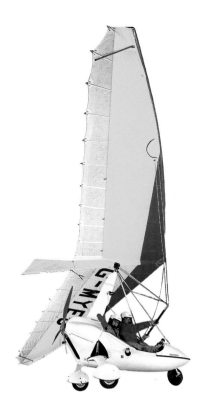

Library of Congress Cataloging-in-Publication Data
Farndon, John.
Machines/ John Farndon. — 1st Amer. ed.
p. cm. — (Picturepedia)
Includes index.
ISBN 1-56458-384-8
1. Machinery—Juvenile literature. [1. Machinery.] I. Title.
II. Series.
TJ147.F37 1994
621.8—dc20
93-20841
CIP
AC

Reproduced by Colourscan, Singapore
Printed and bound in Italy by Graphicom

MACHINES

DK

CONTENTS

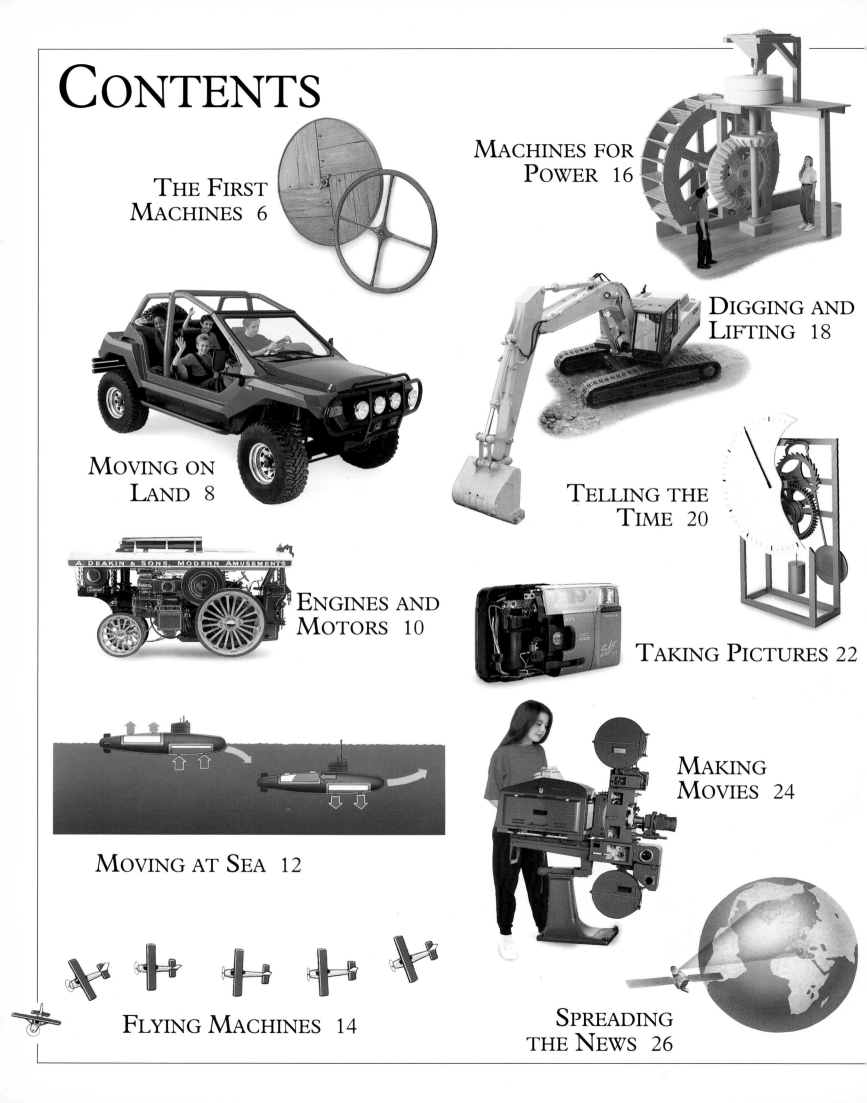

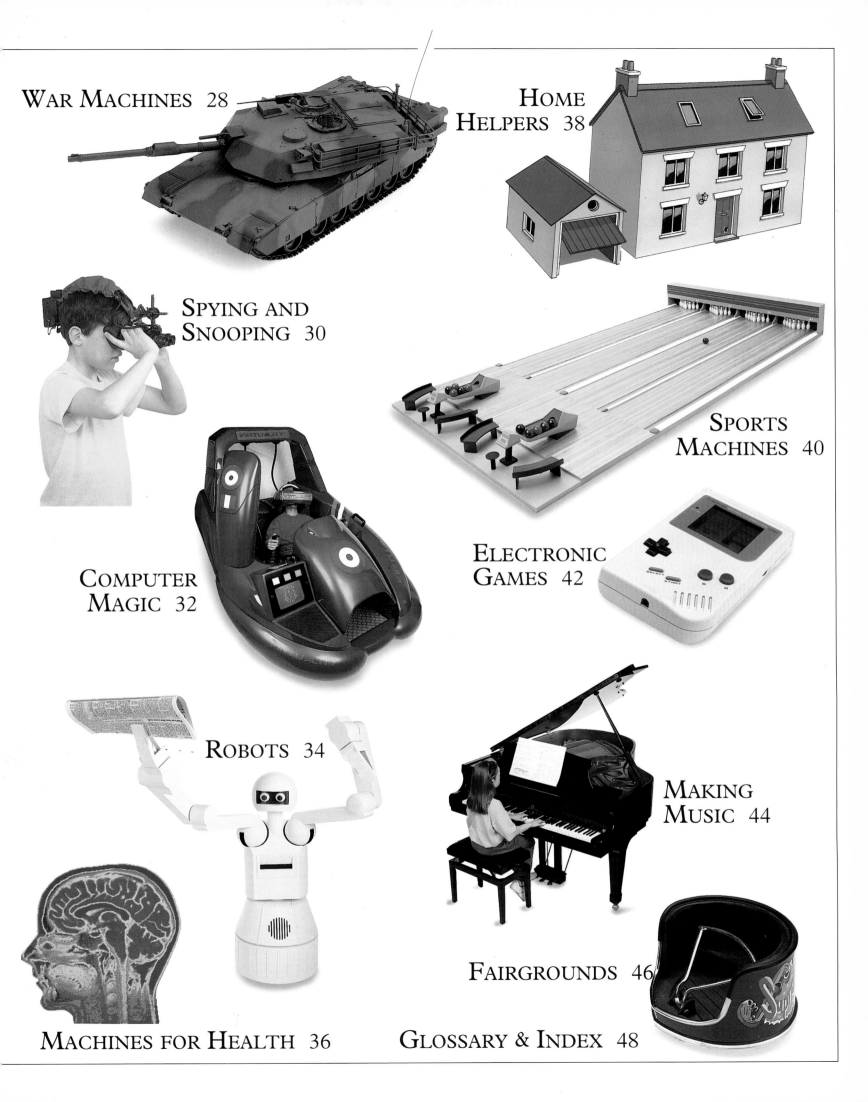

THE FIRST MACHINES

People have always looked for ways of making it easier to do a task. Machines make it possible to do a task using less effort. Over 20,000 years ago, hunters invented the bow and arrow. Armed with this machine, they could send a pointed spear through the air. Other machines followed. The plow was invented about 9,000 years ago, then the wheel. From scissors to screwdrivers, machines are all around us now, making our lives easier.

Bow and Arrow
The first bows were strips of wood bent into a curve with a string. When the archer pulled back the string, the wood bent so much that it sprang back as soon as he let go, shooting the arrow forward.

Roll On
Wheels were invented about 5,000 years ago and were very heavy. Now they are lighter. Modern wheels are suitable for high-speed driving.

The earliest wheeled vehicles had wheels made either of solid wood or of planks, so they were very heavy. They appeared in Mesopotamia over 5,000 years ago.

The Plow
Early people used to turn over the soil for planting with just a digging stick and hoe. But they eventually realized that they could turn the soil much more easily by drawing a cutting blade, called a plow, through it.

The Potter's Wheel
Wheels are used in many machines other than vehicles. In fact, the first wheels were probably used 8,000 years ago by potters for turning clay to make pots, and by millers to grind corn.

The wheels used on ancient Egyptian chariots were much lighter because large sections of wood were cut away.

For thousands of years, most wheels were like this cartwheel. Its wooden spokes were surrounded by a hoop of wood, strengthened by a metal rim.

Helpful Levers
A lever is a machine that puts out more effort than you put in. When you use a pair of scissors, your effort on the handle turns the blades around the hinge, or fulcrum. This magnifies your effort, giving the blades enough power to cut.

A wrench is a lever for turning a bolt very forcefully. The bolt is the fulcrum.

The top of a faucet is a lever that screws up and down to control the flow of water.

The handle of a screwdriver is a lever to help you turn a screw with extra force.

Now all cars have light metal wheels with pneumatic, or air-filled, tires. These give a much softer ride.

Racing cars have very wide tires, called slicks, to give extra grip at high speeds.

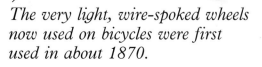

The very light, wire-spoked wheels now used on bicycles were first used in about 1870.

MOVING ON LAND

A 19th-century horse-drawn carriage

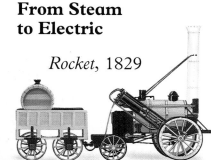

Trevithick's carriage

Once, the only way to travel far on land was on horseback or in a horse-drawn carriage. But in 1803, Englishman Richard Trevithick built a carriage that ran on rails and was driven along by a steam engine. Motorcars first appeared in the 1860s, when gasoline engines were invented. Now there are enough cars in the world to form a traffic jam stretching to the Moon and back!

Turning the Wheels

The axle turns a car's wheels. When a car turns left, the wheels on the right must travel farther than the wheels on the left, so they must turn faster. The engine is connected to the axle by a set of gears, called the differential. This lets the wheels turn at slightly different speeds around corners.

Drive from the engine

Differential

Axle

As in many cars made to be driven off the road, the engine powers all four wheels.

Underneath the hood is a very powerful engine.

These bars protect the passengers if the car crashes and rolls over. Safety belts keep the passengers in.

The chunky tires covered with big knobs are ideal for a good grip in mud and sand.

From Steam to Electric

Rocket, 1829

American steam locomotive, 1875

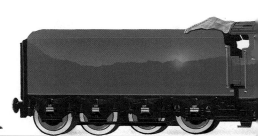

Slippery Cars

Car designers test their designs in wind tunnels to make sure the air flows smoothly over them. A good design uses less gasoline. Wind tunnels use a big fan to create a strong wind. Ribbons stuck to the car show how the wind flows over it.

The Model T Ford was the first car to sell over a million.

Fun Car

Not many cars are as much fun as this dune buggy. But most cars work in much the same way, with an engine at the front to drive the wheels around.

The Volkswagen Beetle was the most popular car ever made. Over 40 million were built.

The City of Truro was the first steam train to reach 100 miles (160 km) an hour.

These headlights help the driver see at night. They must be aimed down to prevent them from dazzling oncoming drivers.

The TGV is the fastest train in the world. It can travel at over 185 miles (300 km) an hour.

Diesel-electric locomotive, 1956

The Mallard, 1938

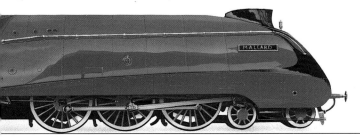

ENGINES AND MOTORS

Engines and motors provide power to make things move. Motors usually run on electricity and drive small things, like hair dryers. Engines are usually more powerful and run on heat. In steam engines – the first real engines – heat boils water to make steam, and the steam pushes the engine around, just as steam in a pan of boiling water pushes up the lid. Cars have "internal combustion" engines. In these, the engine is pushed around by pressure produced from burning gasoline inside the engine.

Boiler to make steam

A. DEAKIN & SONS, MODERN AMUSEMENTS

SUPREME

Letting Off Steam
Until about 40 years ago, brightly colored steam traction engines like this one were often seen at fairgrounds. The traction engine drove the rides and made electricity for the lights.

Electric Power
Electric motors work by magnetism. An electric current passing through a coil of wire turns the coil into a very powerful magnet. If the coil is set between another magnet, it is driven around at great speed to power your hair dryer.

Magnet

The coil of wire spins around.

Jet Power
Most modern airplanes have jet engines. These push a blast of hot air out the back, which drives the plane forward at very high speed.

Gasoline Engine

This is a model of an internal combustion engine, just like those used in most cars today. Fuel is constantly drawn into the engine's cylinder, where it is fired by an electric spark. The explosion pushes the piston down and turns the engine.

Fuel is drawn into the engine through this inlet pipe.

This is the cylinder where the fuel is burned.

This is the spark plug that lights the fuel.

Old, burned fuel is pushed out through this exhaust pipe.

This is the piston. It has been pushed down by the burning fuel.

Cooling fins

Spot the Engine

You can find a machine's engine in all kinds of places. The engines here are colored green.

This is the crankshaft. It turns around and around as the piston goes up and down.

Four Steps

In most cars, the engine works in four steps, which is why it is called a four-stroke engine.

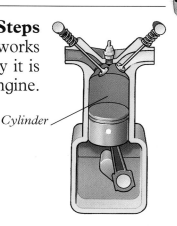

Cylinder

1. Fuel and air pass into the cylinder.

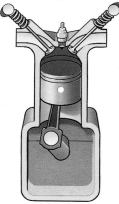

2. The fuel and air are compressed.

Spark plug

3. The spark sets fire to the fuel.

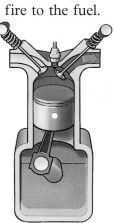

4. The burned gases are pushed out.

Electric car

Magnet-powered train

Propeller aircraft

Jet plane

MOVING AT SEA

Early Sailing Ships

For thousands of years, ships used only the wind to drive them along. Big ships had tall masts with enormous sails. Now many people use sailing boats just for fun.

Early ships, with only the wind to drive them along, were rather slow. And even the biggest of them looks small to us today. But modern ships have powerful engines, and some, supertankers, are so long that the crew needs motor scooters to get from one end to the other. Water covers three-quarters of the Earth's surface, so it is not surprising to find so many different boats and ships all over the world.

Why Don't Ships Sink?

Even though they are heavy, ships float because their hulls are hollow and full of air. A ball of modeling clay sinks, but if you hollow it into a bowl shape, it will float.

A ball of clay sinks.

A bowl of clay floats.

The SeaCat is steered by a pair of water jets on each side.

There are two engines in each of the side hulls.

Going Down!

A submarine dives by pushing air out of and taking water into special tanks. The water makes the submarine so heavy, it sinks.

Coming Up!

It comes up again by taking compressed air into the tanks to force the water out. The submarine gets lighter and floats up.

Cars are stowed on one of the lower decks.

Big Cats

A catamaran's two hulls help it go faster than ordinary boats. The SeaCat is the largest high-speed catamaran. It takes 450 people and 80 cars across the 22 miles (35 km) of the English Channel in under an hour.

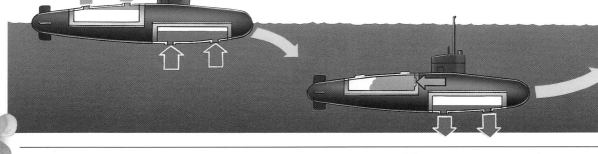

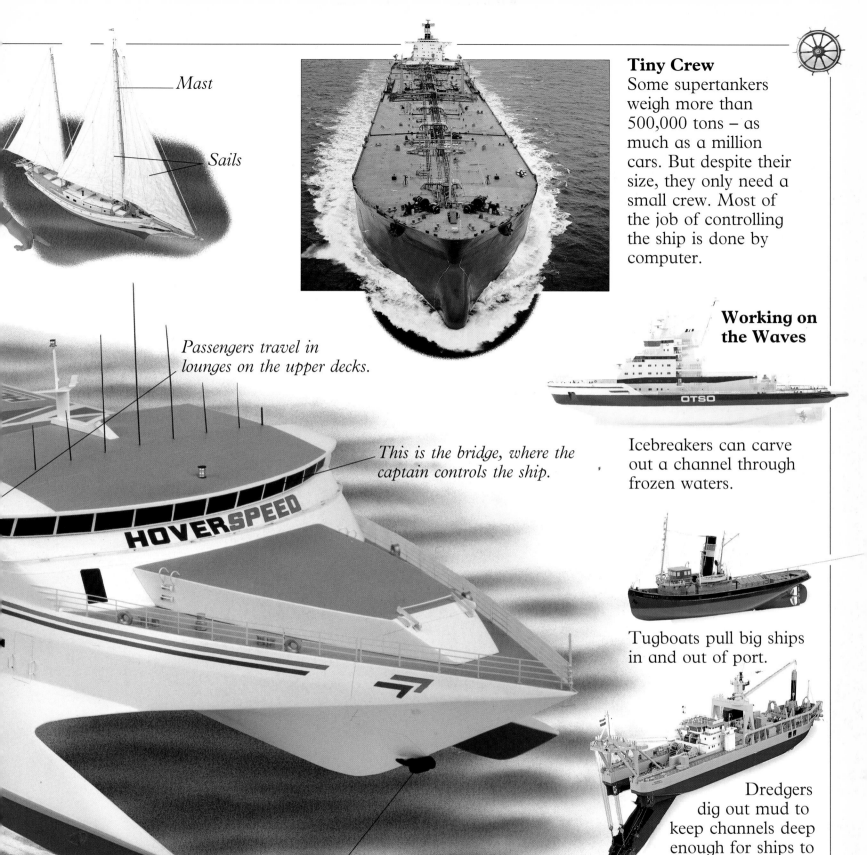

Mast

Sails

Tiny Crew
Some supertankers weigh more than 500,000 tons – as much as a million cars. But despite their size, they only need a small crew. Most of the job of controlling the ship is done by computer.

Working on the Waves

Passengers travel in lounges on the upper decks.

This is the bridge, where the captain controls the ship.

Icebreakers can carve out a channel through frozen waters.

Tugboats pull big ships in and out of port.

Dredgers dig out mud to keep channels deep enough for ships to pass safely.

The SeaCat's long, narrow aluminum hulls cut through the water to make it go faster. Its cruising speed of 35 knots makes the SeaCat as fast as the fastest-ever passenger liner.

The SeaCat's anchor is attached to the third, central hull. This hull only comes into use in rough weather.

Tankers carry oil all over the world.

FLYING MACHINES

The simplest flying machine of all is a kite, which is swept up into the air by a strong wind. People were lifted off the ground by big kites in China over 3,000 years ago! But kites only go where the wind blows. To fly where you want to go, you must have an engine to drive you along and a means of steering.

Light, fabric wing

Battens to stiffen the wing

This is an ultralight – the smallest airplane of all.

Lighter than Air
Hot-air balloons have a big bag of light material that is filled with hot air. This air is so light it rises, lifting the balloon as it goes. The height of the balloon in the sky is controlled by a gas burner. Heating the air inside the balloon makes it rise. If you let the air cool, the balloon will sink.

The wing is pushed up.

Air flowing past the wing

How Wings Work
The wings of a plane are specially shaped so that the air zooms over and under them at great speed. This lifts the wings, just as wind lifts a kite.

The propeller is turned by a small gas engine.

Gas burner

Basket to carry passengers

The back wheels are on springs so that landing is not too bumpy.

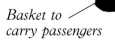

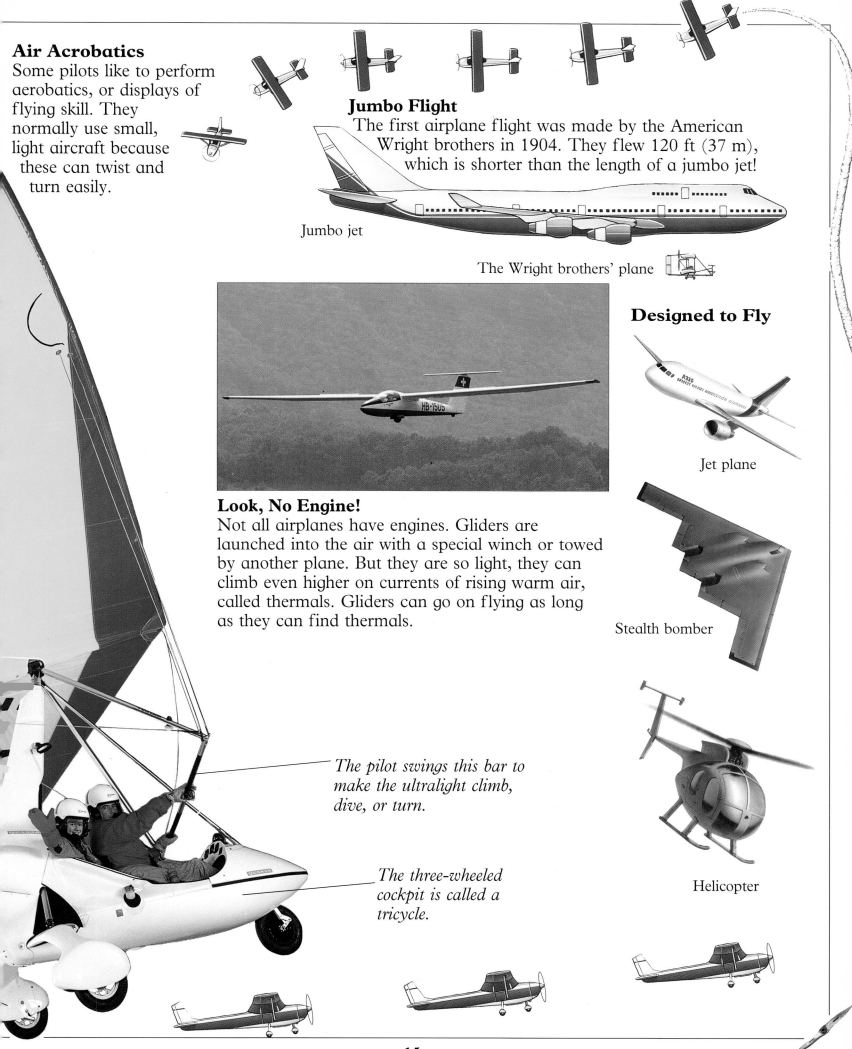

Air Acrobatics

Some pilots like to perform aerobatics, or displays of flying skill. They normally use small, light aircraft because these can twist and turn easily.

Jumbo Flight

The first airplane flight was made by the American Wright brothers in 1904. They flew 120 ft (37 m), which is shorter than the length of a jumbo jet!

Jumbo jet

The Wright brothers' plane

Designed to Fly

Jet plane

Stealth bomber

Look, No Engine!

Not all airplanes have engines. Gliders are launched into the air with a special winch or towed by another plane. But they are so light, they can climb even higher on currents of rising warm air, called thermals. Gliders can go on flying as long as they can find thermals.

The pilot swings this bar to make the ultralight climb, dive, or turn.

The three-wheeled cockpit is called a tricycle.

Helicopter

MACHINES FOR POWER

Wheat pours through this hopper onto the grindstone below.

The sails of a windmill are turned by the wind, just as a toy pinwheel turns when you blow on it. The wheel of a water mill is turned by a stream rushing past it. Windmills and water mills were the power stations of the past, providing the power needed for big or tiring tasks, like cutting stone or grinding wheat. Now we use wind and water power to make electricity, and the electricity drives the machines that do jobs like these for us.

1. The waterwheel has paddles that dip into the stream. The rushing water pushes on the paddles and turns the wheel.

Air Power
Windmills use the wind to drive their machinery. The top of this mill can be turned so that the sails are always facing the wind.

2. As the waterwheel goes around, it turns a long rod or axle.

Water Power

Most water mills ground wheat into flour, but they were also used for crushing olives, cutting marble, or even mashing rags into paper.

6. These big, flat stones are called grindstones. The upper one is turned by the main shaft. As it turns, the wheat is crushed to flour between the two grindstones.

5. This is the main shaft. As the crown wheel turns, the main shaft turns with it.

4. This is the crown wheel. As the brake wheel turns, its teeth push the grooves of the crown wheel and turn it around.

3. Turning at the end of the axle is the brake wheel. All around its edge are teeth that slot into matching grooves on the crown wheel.

Gas Power

In gas-fired power stations, gas is burned to drive machines that make electricity.

Atom Power

In nuclear power stations, heat to make electricity comes from splitting atoms.

These gear wheels are connected by teeth that slot into each other.

These gear wheels are connected by a belt.

All Geared Up

Pairs of special wheels, called gears, can make machines go more slowly, more quickly, or more powerfully. If a small wheel turns a big wheel, the big wheel goes more slowly than the small one because it has farther to go around.

Strong Currents

Hydroelectric power is electricity made from rivers. The river water is collected behind a wall, or dam. Gates open to let the water rush into a tunnel, where it turns special wheels that make the electricity. A lot of hydroelectric power is produced in countries with large rivers and high mountains.

DIGGING AND LIFTING

When you build a sand castle on the beach, you only need a tiny shovel to dig out the sand. But to build factories, office buildings, bridges, or tunnels, you need huge digging and lifting machines. Some are bigger than houses. Most have powerful arms and levers moved by hydraulics, and some are controlled by computers and guided by lasers.

Tunnel Giant
The tunnel linking England and France is 33 miles (53.1 km) long and passes 132 feet (40 m) under the bed of the English Channel. Two machines, each 755 feet (230 m) long, were specially built in order to dig the tunnel.

Powerful hydraulic rams push the head forward and steer the machine.

A conveyor belt carries the rock that is cut away out to the back of the machine.

Special rams push concrete linings into place to keep the rock from falling in.

To make the Channel tunnel, two of these boring machines, one at each end of the tunnel, slowly cut toward each other. They were guided by lasers so that they met in the middle.

How Hydraulics Works

The arm of this power shovel is moved hydraulically. A pipe along the arm is filled with a special oil. When a piston pushes on the oil in one end of the pipe, the oil pushes another piston out at the far end with much greater force – enough to move the arm and its huge load.

Hydraulic piston

The bucket carves out the earth.

Wide tracks stop the power shovel from slipping and keep it stable.

Up and Away

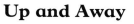

Forklift

Dump truck

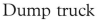

Bulldozer

Towering Cranes

Tall cranes have a system of wheels, called pulleys, which means they can lift very heavy weights.

The cutting head has very hard teeth to cut through the rock. It turns around and around to grind the rock away.

Backhoe

TELLING THE TIME

Early clocks were not very accurate. Their gears were turned by a falling weight attached to an "escape" wheel. The escape wheel made sure that the gears only moved, or "escaped," a little at a time. But the weight did not always fall at the same speed. So a pendulum, with its regular swing, was added to keep the escape wheel turning at a regular speed. In a modern clock, the steady beat that moves the gears comes from the vibrations of a piece of quartz crystal.

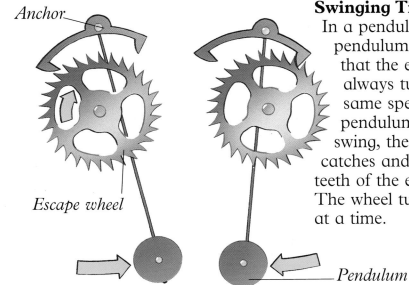

Anchor

Escape wheel

Pendulum

Swinging Time
In a pendulum clock, the pendulum makes sure that the escape wheel always turns at the same speed. With the pendulum's regular swing, the anchor on top catches and releases the teeth of the escape wheel. The wheel turns, one tooth at a time.

Pendulum Clock
This is a model of a very simple pendulum clock. It only has an hour hand, so it is simpler inside than a real clock.

Clock face

This heavy weight keeps the clock going. It is wound up to the top of the cable with a handle. The weight then falls slowly down again, pulling the escape wheel around as it goes.

Sun Time
As the sun moves through the sky, the shadows it casts move, too. Long before clocks were invented, people used to tell the time by looking at the position of shadows. You can see this for yourself if you plant a stick in the ground and mark where its shadow falls at various times of day.

This is the hour hand. If a minute hand were on this clock, too, it would need its own gear wheel to turn it at a different speed from the hour hand.

The anchor on the swinging pendulum controls the turning escape wheel.

This is the escape wheel. It turns the main gear wheel.

The main gear wheel moves the hour hand around.

The pendulum swings back and forth with a regular beat.

Crystal Time

When an electric current from a battery is sent through tiny crystals of a rock called quartz, the crystals vibrate very quickly. The vibrations are too small to see, but they are so regular that they are used to keep time in very accurate quartz watches.

Crystal of quartz

The Big Time

One of the most accurate of all pendulum clocks is the clock in the tower of Big Ben in London.

Past Time

Before clocks with gears and pendulums were invented, people used all kinds of systems to keep track of time.

Water clock   Candle clock   Oil clock

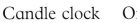

Star clock

TAKING PICTURES

Inside a camera is a roll of film that records all your photos one by one in a long strip. When you press the button to take a picture, a little door, or shutter, in the camera clicks open for a split second, letting light in to shine on the film. Special chemicals on the film record the pattern of light to make the picture.

The autofocus measures how far away the subject of your photograph is and adjusts the lens automatically.

The viewfinder is a window through the camera to help you aim correctly.

Light rays from the object in front of the camera pass through the lens. They reach the film to make a picture or "image" on it.

The button you press to open the shutter and take a picture is called the shutter release.

This counter tells you how many pictures you have taken.

Instant Pictures
Polaroid cameras can give you pictures almost instantly. This is because all the chemicals needed to develop the photo are stored in a bulge at the end of each section of film.

You take your picture.

The picture is pushed out through rollers that squeeze the chemicals from the bulge over the paper.

As the chemicals get to work, the picture starts to appear.

After a minute or two, the picture is ready.

The flash adds extra light to make sure the subject you are photographing is bright enough.

Magic Holograms
Normal photographs are completely flat and look the same from any angle. But with holograms, made using laser light, the view changes as you move the picture – just as it would in real life.

On Credit
Holograms on credit cards make it more difficult for people to make illegal copies of the cards.

SENSOR FLASH

AUTO FOCUS

AF 2

OPEN

The lens concentrates the light on the film.

Hot Spots
You can sometimes leave a camera to take a photo in a place it would be much too dangerous for you to stay – like by an erupting volcano.

NIKONOS-V

HASSELBLAD

500ELX

Seascape
Special waterproof cameras can take pictures under the sea, but it is usually so dark that photographers must use very powerful flash equipment.

Moonstruck
In 1969, astronauts took special cameras to the Moon to take pictures of the Moon's surface.

MAKING MOVIES

When you watch a movie, people and things on the screen seem to move as naturally as if they were real. Yet what you are seeing is actually a series of thousands of still photographs, or "frames." But the frames change so quickly, it is as if the people and things are moving. If the projector – the machine that shines the film onto the screen – were slowed down, you would see each of these still photographs going past, one by one.

Reel Life
Even a reel of film lasting just a few minutes has many thousands of pictures. Each picture is very small, but the projector magnifies it to fill the movie screen.

As the film passes through the projector, a light shines through the frames, one by one, projecting them onto the screen.

Shutter open

Gate

Moving the Film
In a movie camera, there is a special shutter. This turns to let light reach the film, one frame at a time, as the film runs quickly through the gate.

Shutter closed

Each time the shutter closes, a swinging claw slots into a hole along the side of the film and pulls the next frame into position. Projectors have a similar claw to move the film through.

Swinging claw

Film is stored in circular cans.

Moving Dinosaurs

Weird creatures in TV shows like "The Dinosaurs" can be a lot of fun to watch. They look realistic but in fact are latex models. Computer-controlled electric motors inside them make the models move just like real-life animals.

When the dinosaur smiles, a computer instructs dozens of little electric motors to move different parts of his face.

© The Walt Disney Company

Editing a Film

When a movie is shot, the sound is recorded on special, separate tapes. The editor uses an editing table to make sure that the pictures and sounds match when film and sound are put together.

The film starts on this reel.

Screen to view pictures

Spool of film with pictures

Loudspeaker

Spool with recorded speech

Spool with recorded sound effects

Disaster!

Filmmakers can use special effects to create the weather they want or to make dangerous things happen safely. Here, gas jets shoot out flames that make it look as if a building is being burned down.

A lens magnifies the picture so that it fills the screen.

Every second, 24 frames pass through the projector.

As the movie is shown, the film is gradually wound onto the take-up reel.

The Big Screen

You can watch a film on the big screen at a theater or on a small home-movie screen in your living room. The pictures you see are actually the reflected images of the pictures on the film. The light in the projector throws the images onto the screen.

The screen is usually made of special white material to make the picture bright and clear.

25

WAR MACHINES

An aircraft carrier

Hand grenade

Modern armies have all kinds of weapons, from rifles and grenades for fighting a single enemy, to bombs and missiles for attacking large targets. Soldiers can go into battle riding in a tank – a huge gun on wheels protected by heavy armor plating. But nothing can protect against nuclear bombs, the most powerful weapons of all.

Going Bang!

Gunpowder was first used in China about 1,000 years ago for making fireworks.

In 1605, Guy Fawkes tried to blow up the English Parliament with gunpowder.

In 1867, Alfred Nobel invented a very powerful explosive, called dynamite.

The main gun can fire powerful shells that will travel 9,900 ft (3,000 m).

This is the turret. It turns around so the gun can be aimed in any direction.

The tank can carry a huge amount of fuel – around 500 gallons (1,900 liters). But it is only enough to drive about 270 miles (440 km) at 25 miles (40 km) an hour.

The commander sits at the top.

The driver sits inside at the front and uses mirrors to see what is happening outside.

The gunner aims the main gun using a thermal-imaging sight. This picks up the heat given off by enemy targets.

The loader loads the main gun with explosive shells and also operates the radio.

Runway at Sea

Aircraft carriers are huge ships with flat decks, which warplanes use for taking off and landing. The carriers sail close to enemy coasts so the planes can launch attacks.

One of the crew uses a machine gun to defend the tank against enemy aircraft.

Heavy steel armor up to 5 inches (13 cm) thick protects the crew from enemy fire.

Best Shot

Muskets were used by soldiers in the 17th century. They needed reloading after each shot.

Handguns like this Colt 45 were carried about 150 years ago by cowboys in the American west. They could fire six bullets without being reloaded.

Machine guns were invented in 1884 by Sir Hiram Maxim. They could fire dozens of bullets one after the other.

The wheels run inside tough metal bands, called caterpillar tracks. To steer, the driver makes one track run faster than the other.

Destruction caused by a nuclear bomb in Hiroshima, Japan, 1945

Nuclear Weapons

A single nuclear bomb can destroy a whole city, and the radiation it leaves behind can kill people and animals years later. There are now enough nuclear weapons to destroy the world.

A Nuclear Explosion

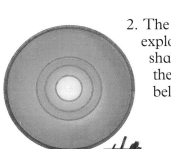

1. As the bomb explodes, it makes a giant fireball.

2. The explosion shakes the city below.

3. The blast and fire destroy buildings.

4. Rubble and dust mushroom up high into the sky.

SPYING AND SNOOPING

Spies make it their business to find out other people's secrets, and they have an array of sneaky devices to help them. Tiny radio transmitters, or "bugs," can be hidden in a room to listen in on private conversations. Video recorders can be concealed in books and briefcases to take pictures without anyone knowing. There are special goggles and cameras to spot things in the dark, and if you think someone is cheating you, there are clever gadgets to help you find out.

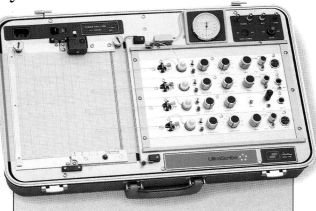

Are You Lying?
Lying often makes people sweat more or breathe more quickly, or makes their heart beat faster. Liars can often be caught by using a lie detector to spot these changes.

I Spy
Two people meet to chat in an ordinary room. But is it an ordinary room? Is it an ordinary conversation? There is more here than meets the eye.

Green fingers? Hidden in the plant pot is a tiny tape recorder to record the conversation with your visitor.

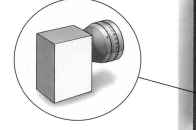

Can you read between the lines? No bigger than an eraser, this video camera can be slipped inside a book for secret filming.

Is she tricking you? A voice-stress analyzer hidden in the desk may alert you to telltale tremors in her voice.

It looks like an ordinary briefcase. In fact it is a secret video recorder. The lens is a tiny hole in the side, and the controls to start recording are in the handle.

Are you receiving me? Your boss can give you instructions without anyone knowing, using an ear spy – a tiny radio receiver that fits invisibly inside your ear.

Fact or Fantasy?

In the fantasy world of spy films, anything can happen. James Bond's car could squirt oil or fire tacks from the rear lights. A bullet-proof panel helped protect him, extendable bumpers could ram other cars, and radar in the rear-view mirrors kept track of enemy cars.

The lighter patches show the warm engines of the cars that arrived most recently at this parking lot.

Seeing Red

A thermal-imaging camera spots warm things, even in the dark. It shows in color the invisible infrared rays given off when something gets hot. The lighter the color, the warmer the object being viewed.

If you are discovered and your enemy has a gun, the bullet-proof vest hidden under your clothes may save your life.

Hidden inside the door knob is a tiny "bug" that picks up all sounds in the room and radios them back to base.

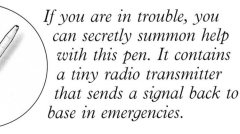

If you are in trouble, you can secretly summon help with this pen. It contains a tiny radio transmitter that sends a signal back to base in emergencies.

A view through night-vision goggles

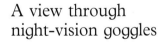

Cat's Eyes

You can see in the dark with these special night-vision goggles, which pick up even the tiniest traces of light.

COMPUTER MAGIC

Computers are the world's smartest machines. Inside a computer are thousands of very tiny electronic switches. By switching these on and off in different combinations, computers can perform all kinds of tasks. They are used every day in car factories, hospitals, supermarkets, and offices. Some guide aircraft, ships, submarines, and spacecraft. Other kinds, such as virtual-reality machines, are used for fun and can take you on exciting imaginary voyages.

The headset has a mini TV screen in front of each eye and a speaker over each ear.

When you move your head, this cable sends signals to the computer.

In a virtual-reality machine, you can imagine you are at the controls of a jet, a spacecraft, or even a mechanical dinosaur.

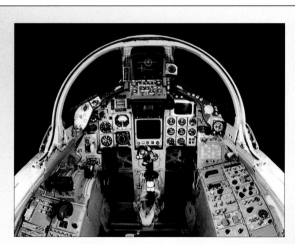

Keeping Your Head Up
Jet fighter pilots must not take their eyes off the view ahead, even for a second. All the information a pilot needs to control the plane and fire at targets is fed to a computer and projected onto the pilot's face mask. This is called a "head-up" display.

Feeling the Way
Doctors can use virtual-reality gloves to look inside you before they decide to operate. As they run their hands over you, sensors in the gloves send signals to a computer. The computer makes a 3-D picture of your insides on a little TV screen in the doctors' headsets.

This cable carries signals from the computer for the pictures and sounds in the headset.

When you turn your head, different views come up on the TV screens in the headset.

Pocket Brain
Fifty years ago, the first computers filled a large room. Now an equally clever computer can be the same size as a pocket calculator.

Bytes and Megabytes
Computers can help with homework or get an astronaut to the Moon.

Calculator

Laptop computer

Shrinking Switches
The switches in computers have got steadily smaller and more complicated.

The first computers had big glass valves.

Personal computer

Computers now have tiny microchips.

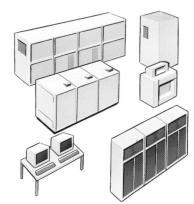

Super computer

Electric motors rock the virtual-reality machine backward and forward and from side to side to make your "journey" more realistic.

ROBOTS

Robots are machines that "think" with a computer brain that tells them what to do.
Once they have been programmed, they can work entirely by themselves. Some people believe that one day we will be able to make robots that can do everything a human can – and they may even look like humans. At the moment, though, most robots are nothing more than mechanical arms or cranes.

Mechanical Humans

Automatons are machines that move rather like humans or animals. This one was made for a fair in Victorian times.

Factory Hand

A factory robot is often just a moving arm. But a robotic arm can hold things, screw them into place, weld them, and check that they work. It can replace lots of human workers.

An electronic voice allows the robot to answer and ask simple questions. It can also obey some clearly spoken commands.

Robots at Work and Play

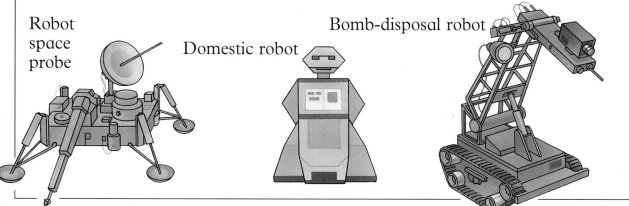

Robot space probe

Domestic robot

Bomb-disposal robot

Robotic arm

The robot can pick up your newspaper by squeezing its claws together. Its "muscles" are powered by electric motors.

Each of the claws has special pressure sensors so that they do not crush things they pick up.

Electronic eyes allow the robot to spot obstacles in its path and steer around them.

The robot's brain is a powerful computer. It tells the robot what to do by sending electronic signals to the motors that move the robot's different parts.

Robogymnast
The robot can turn its hands and move its arms. But unlike a human, it can turn its arms completely around.

It can also turn at the waist or swivel on its base.

Home Help
A robot like this is really just a clever toy. But one day there may be robots that can do the shopping, cleaning, and other household chores for you.

Like Humans?
Manny is a lifelike robot with computers that can make it "sweat" and "breathe." Scientists use Manny to test special clothing, like space suits and fire-fighting clothes. If Manny can "breathe" and doesn't "sweat" too much, then the clothes will be safe for a human to wear.

Manny has joints that move just like a human's.

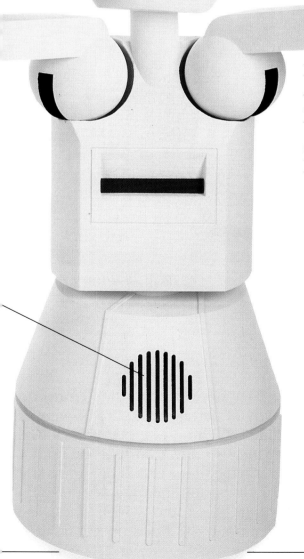

MACHINES FOR HEALTH

This is an MRI scan that has had colors added.

If you have to visit your doctor or go to the hospital, you will see that doctors use lots of machines to help them find out what is wrong with you. There are simple machines to check your blood pressure or listen to your chest. There are also some really complicated ones, like the huge electronic scanning machines, which can take pictures of the inside of the body – showing anything from a baby growing in its mother's womb to what goes on in your brain.

First Sounds

A pregnant woman may be given ultrasound scans to see how her baby is growing. These use sounds that are too high for us to hear. When the sounds are beamed into the mother's womb, a computer analyzes the way they are reflected to create a picture of the baby inside.

The patient can be moved backward and forward on the sliding table for different parts of the body to be viewed.

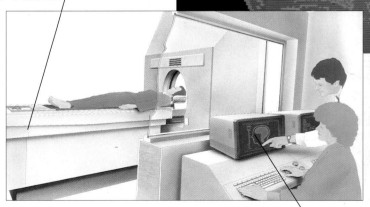

The image is displayed on a computer screen.

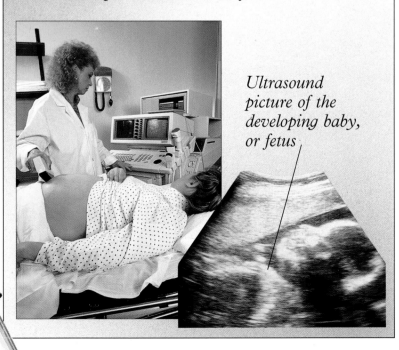

Ultrasound picture of the developing baby, or fetus

Magnetic Resonance Imaging

MRI is a safe way of getting a picture of what is going on inside someone. The patient lies in a ring of magnets so powerful that the body's atoms are pulled into line. The atoms are knocked briefly out of line by a strong radio signal and send out little radio waves. These are used by a computer to build up the picture.

Look Inside?

Doctors use many instruments to see inside you and check if there is anything the matter.

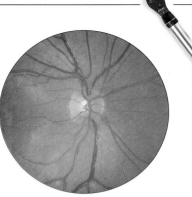

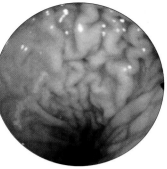

Stomach viewed with an endoscope

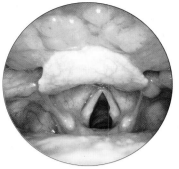

Vocal cords viewed with a laryngoscope

Inside of the eye viewed with an ophthalmoscope

Listening In

A stethoscope is a listening tube. With it, a doctor can hear the sounds made by your heart and lungs. It will help the doctor decide what is wrong with you.

X-Ray Vision

X rays are a bit like light rays, but they pass through skin as easily as light shines through glass. They do not pass through bones, though, so an X-ray picture shows the shadows of bones. Your dentist might take an X ray of your teeth to see if they are growing correctly.

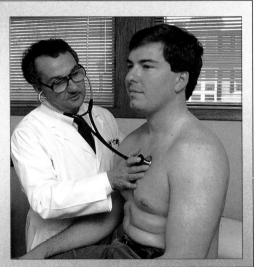

This X ray of a boy's second teeth shows he has tooth decay.

Brain Slice

MRI gives doctors very clear pictures. It can be used to spot heart problems and abnormal growths in the brain so that they can be operated on.

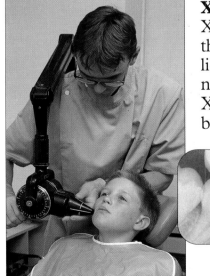

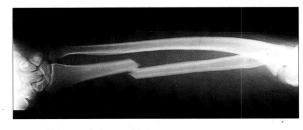

X-Ray Arm

By looking at this X-ray picture of a broken arm, the doctor can see exactly where the damage is and can decide how to treat it.

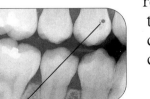

HOME HELPERS

Before gas and electricity, people used open fires to cook and keep warm by, read by candlelight, and got down on their hands and knees to clean the carpet. Now, in many parts of the world, homes and gardens are full of machines that make life easier, safer, and more comfortable. With the time we save doing household chores, we can groom ourselves from top to toe with a choice of electrical gadgets.

Outdoor lights with sensors can turn themselves on when someone comes near. Burglars beware!

You can plug a special vacuum cleaner into a socket in each room. The dust is sucked away through hidden pipes to a waste bin.

Power Gardening

There are lots of machines to help in the garden. Weed trimmers cut weeds and grass in awkward corners, hedge trimmers take the effort out of keeping a hedge tidy, and chain saws are for sawing large branches. Robot lawn mowers can cut the grass automatically.

As you drive up to your garage, you can press a button in your car to open the electronically controlled garage door.

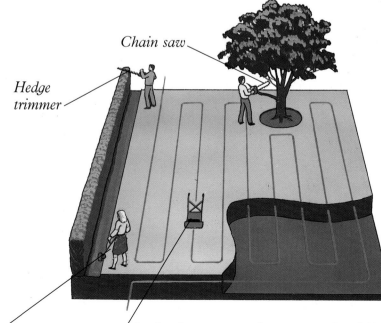

Chain saw

Hedge trimmer

Weed strimmer

A robot lawn mower has sensors that follow a cable buried under the lawn. The mower cuts the grass automatically as it follows the cable.

Your cat can wear a special tag on its collar. The tag opens the cat door for it – but keeps strange cats firmly locked out.

Smoke detectors set off an alarm to warn if there is smoke in your home. They can help you stop a fire from spreading.

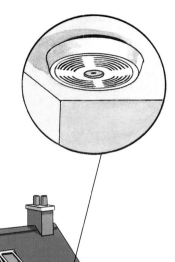

In Control
Thermostats in greenhouses keep plants at the right temperature because plants, like people, do not like to be too hot or too cold. A thermostat turns the heat off if it gets too warm, and on if it gets too cold.

This timer controls the central heating. It automatically switches the heating on and off at whatever times you want during the day.

Time for Yourself
There are all kinds of machines you can use to look after yourself. You can curl your hair with a curling iron and clean your teeth with an electric toothbrush. Some people shave with an electric razor, tone their muscles with electronic slimming pads, then round off their tiring day using an electric foot massager.

Gadgets Galore
There are many machines for cooking and cleaning in the average house.

Refrigerator

Washing machine

Electric stove

Coffee machine

Sports Machines

In the past, sports were rather simple. Often, a bat and ball were all you needed. Today there are many fantastic sports machines. In bowling alleys, machines reset the pins after each throw. On tennis courts, machines check electronically where the balls bounce. On mountainsides, machines make artificial snow for skiers. Even fencing, which used to be for killing an enemy, is now a sport with electric equipment to help judge who is the winner.

Finger holes in the ball make it easier to grip.

Display screens tell you how many pins you have knocked down and give the score.

Most bowling alleys have lots of lanes so that many people can play at once.

Making Snow
People love playing in snow – but sometimes there just isn't enough of it. Many ski resorts have machines to make artificial snow for skiers. These snow machines use a special cold gas that turns water into powdery ice. The ice is pumped out through a nozzle onto the slopes.

On the Line
Electronic sensors buried beneath the lines on a tennis court can tell if a ball bounces inside the court. The ball is coated with iron powder, and the sensors detect it as it passes over. If the ball is out, a signal goes off.

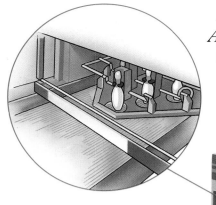
After each ball, the pins that have been bowled over are cleared away. Automatic grips hold the others in place.

At the end of your turn, all the pins are cleared away, then set down in exactly the right places, ready for the next bowler.

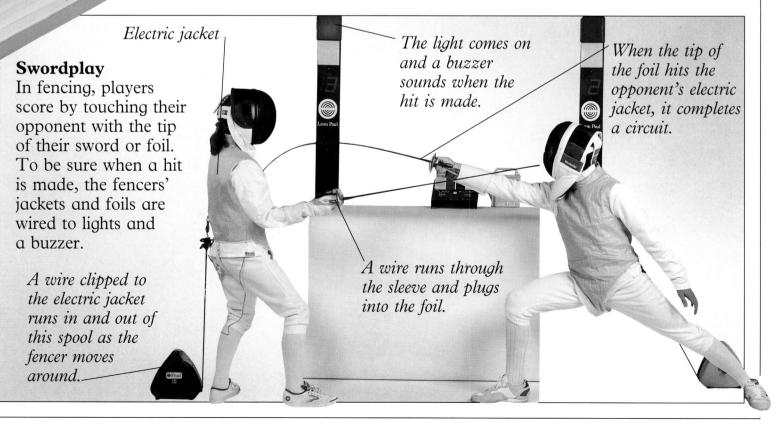

After each throw, the ball automatically returns down a track hidden beneath the surface.

You roll a ball from here toward a set of pins. The aim is to see how many pins you can knock down.

Electric jacket

The light comes on and a buzzer sounds when the hit is made.

When the tip of the foil hits the opponent's electric jacket, it completes a circuit.

Swordplay

In fencing, players score by touching their opponent with the tip of their sword or foil. To be sure when a hit is made, the fencers' jackets and foils are wired to lights and a buzzer.

A wire runs through the sleeve and plugs into the foil.

A wire clipped to the electric jacket runs in and out of this spool as the fencer moves around.

ELECTRONIC GAMES

Remote control

At the heart of every electronic game, there is a tiny block or chip, called a processor. Inside the chip are thousands of little electronic circuits. Whenever a light flashes or a spaceship moves across the game screen, it is the circuits that are making it happen. Some games, like electronic chess, have their circuits set at the factory so the circuits cannot change. But in hand-held video games, you put in a disk, and the disk controls the circuits. Each disk makes the circuits work in a different way and gives you a new game to play.

The custom chip keeps track of the score and controls the screen display.

You press the start button to switch the machine on.

The cross-shaped direction button gives you control over the movement of figures on the screen.

The aerial sends out beams of radio waves to the car.

Remote Control
The controls of a remote-controlled model car, plane, or boat send out beams of radio waves.
A tiny radio on the model picks up the waves and switches on an electric current. The current operates the model's little electric motors, or servos. The servos steer the model or make it go faster or slower.

You press this select button to choose your game and skill level.

The loudspeaker makes the sound effects.

Radio receiver in model

The circuits beneath the liquid crystal display screen make it go dark in certain places. The pattern of light and dark forms the picture.

The processor chip sends a stream of electronic signals to the circuits beneath the screen.

Electronic Toys

Electronics are used in many of the toys you play with. Even a game like chess, which has been around for hundreds of years, can now be played electronically.

Electronic chess

Information from the game disk is fed into the processor chip.

The circuits of the processor chip control the game.

Infrared screen control gun

These buttons control firing, rotating, and jumping.

Tabletop soccer game

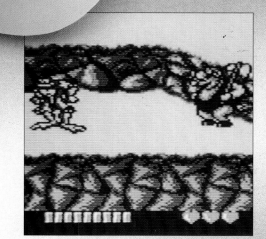

On Display

Video games have an LCD, or liquid crystal display, screen made up of thousands of small squares. Beneath each square is a tiny liquid crystal and a mirror that reflects light. When an electric current is sent through the crystal, the crystal twists and blocks the reflection, making that square dark. The picture is built up from light and dark squares.

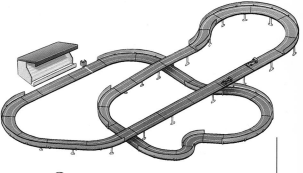

Car-race game

MAKING MUSIC

Over 40,000 years ago, people discovered they could carve animal horns to make musical instruments such as flutes. Since then, thousands of different musical instruments have been created, from simple whistles to grand pianos, each with its own special sound. Now, as well as making music, we can also listen to recorded music anytime we want, thanks to electronic machines like personal stereos and CD players.

The longer strings at this end give deeper notes.

Pressing keys at this end gives very deep notes.

Very Grand Piano
The piano is one of the biggest instruments and one of the most popular. You can use all ten fingers to play ten notes at a time, so its sound can be very dramatic.

These pedals alter the sound slightly, making it softer or louder.

Sounds in the Air
When you play an instrument, the surrounding air is stretched and squeezed again and again. You hear the sound because these squeezings and stretchings – known as sound waves – travel through the air and vibrate your eardrums.

Hammer Action
When you press on a key, a lever lifts a jack. The jack raises a soft-headed hammer that hits a taut metal string, making it vibrate. The string vibrates the air to make the sound we hear.

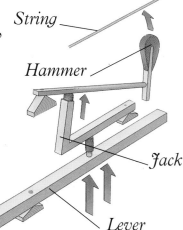

String

Hammer

Jack

Lever

Key

A Museum of Music

Waxed cylinder music player

Phonograph

Reel-to-reel tape recorder

Radio recorder

Portable CD player

The shorter strings at this end give higher notes.

A piano is called a keyboard instrument because you play it by pressing the keys with your fingers.

Pressing keys at this end gives high notes.

The black and white wooden strips are called keys. When you press them, they make the strings inside the piano vibrate.

Electronic Keyboards

An electronic keyboard is played like a piano, but it works very differently. A piano's sound comes from vibrating strings. An electronic keyboard's sound is made with tiny electronic vibrations. It can mimic all kinds of instruments.

Sounds Special

A trumpet is a brass instrument played by blowing with pursed lips.

A recorder is a woodwind instrument played by blowing through a shaped mouthpiece.

A violin is a string instrument played by vibrating the strings with a bow.

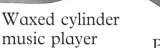

FAIRGROUNDS

A seat or bucket

Fairgrounds are full of colorful, fantastic machines to thrill you and make you laugh. The first big fairground machines were the merry-go-rounds or carousels of about 120 years ago.

These beautiful, steam-driven merry-go-rounds, with gaily painted horses, turned to the sound of an automatic steam-driven organ. The roller coasters, Ferris wheels, and other rides of today are driven by powerful diesel engines or electric motors. Rides get more spectacular and more exciting every day!

A powerful motor in the middle drives the moving floor around.

Colored lights flash on and off as this "waltzer" spins around.

Pinned to Your Seat

When you whirl a ball around on a string, you feel it pulling away. Let go of the string, and the ball will go flying off in a straight line. This effect, called centrifugal force, keeps you in your seat in a roller coaster, even when you are upside down. Just like the ball, your body tries to carry on in a straight line as the car loops around, so you are pressed into your seat.

Centrifugal force keeps pushing the bucket – and you – outward.

The bucket can spin, but is held firmly in place on the floor.

Riding High
It is still possible to find old-fashioned merry-go-rounds with their painted horses, even in a modern fairground.

Roller Coasters
Roller coasters hurtle you up, down, and around in loops. Wheels above and below the track hold the cars in place, and centrifugal force keeps you in your seat – even when you are travelling upside down at 80 miles (130 km) an hour.

All the Fun of the Fair

Ferris wheel

The outer floor of the waltzer stays still.

Teacup ride

The central platform has hinged sections that allow it to bend up and down as it goes around.

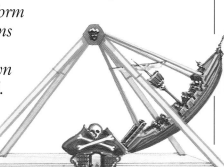

Pirate swingboat

Bright Lights
It needs a lot of electric power to keep fairs brightly lit. Fairgrounds make their own electricity, using noisy, big, diesel-driven generators on trucks.

Dodge'em car

GLOSSARY

Aerial A rod or a loop of wire connected to a TV or radio that picks up signals from the air.

Atom The tiniest bit of a chemical substance. It can only be seen under a very powerful microscope.

Circuit The loop of wire around which an electric current flows.

Combustion A scientific word that means "burning."

Compressed air Air squashed into a small container. It can be let out in a jet strong enough to drive tools like drills.

Computer An electronic machine for processing information. It can do anything, from simple sums to guiding a spacecraft.

Crankshaft In an engine, a rod with a series of right-angled bends, called cranks. As the pistons of the engine go up and down, they turn the crankshaft around and around.

Diesel engine A type of engine often used in trucks and buses. Diesel fuel does not need a spark to set it alight.

Electric current A steady flow of electricity through a wire.

Electronic Controlled by electric circuits that are switched on and off with tiny switches like transistors. Silicon chips are tiny electronic circuits.

Hull The shell of a ship, which sits in the water.

Jack A tool used for lifting heavy things.

Laser An intense, pencil-thin beam of light that can be used for anything from delicate eye surgery to blasting holes through steel.

Lens A specially shaped disk of glass that focuses, or brings together, light rays to form a picture.

Magnet A piece of steel with magnetic power – the invisible force that pulls other magnets toward it or pushes them away.

Meter A tool for measuring things, for example, how much gas you have used.

Microchip A tiny package of complicated electronic circuits. Microchips are the most important part of computers and other electronic devices.

Microphone A device that turns sounds, such as voices, into an electrical signal.

Propeller The whirling blades that drive ships and some airplanes along.

Radar A scanner that sends out a beam of radio signals to find out where ships and airplanes are.

Radiation Energy spreading outwards. Light is a kind of radiation. So are the rays given off by nuclear bombs and nuclear power stations.

Receiver The earpiece on a phone.

Satellite A human-made machine that circles the Earth high up in space. It can bounce TV signals and phone calls around the world or can send pictures of the Earth back for weather forecasts.

Scan A means of building a picture of something by running a beam over each of its parts in turn.

Sensor A machine that detects change, for example, change in heat or pressure.

Space probe A kind of spacecraft sent far off into space under computer and radio control.

Supertanker A giant oil tanker. Supertankers are the biggest ships in the world.

Traction engine An old steam engine used for pulling heavy weights, like plows.

Virtual reality The illusion of reality created by a computer headset.

Acknowledgments

Photography: Steve Gorton, David Rudkin Studios, James Stevenson.

Illustrations: The Colour Company, Roy Flooks, Peter Griffiths, Ray Hutchins, Norman Lacey, Linden Artists, Patrick Mulray, Sebastian Quigly, Peter Serjeant.

Models: Cheltenham Cutaway Exhibits Ltd, Donks Models, Peter Griffiths.

Thanks to: Norrie Carr Child Model Agency; Dakar Cars; Sue Duffey; Mr. A.F. Gueterbock and the Eurotunnel Exhibition Centre; Imperial War Museum; JCB (UK) Ltd; Simon Markson and Markson Pianos; The Old Sarum Flying Club; Leon Paul Equipment Company Ltd; Reuters Televison Ltd; Scallywags Child Model Agency; Sea Containers Services Ltd; Mr. K.J. Selwood; T.L.M; Wessex Microlytes; W. Industries, Leicester, for the loan of a "Virtuality" machine.

Picture credits

Aviation Picture Library: Austin J. Brown 14c, back jacket; **British Aerospace:** 32bl; **Brookes and Vernons/JCB:** 2-3c, 4cra, 18tl, 18bl, 19tc; **Bruce Coleman:** Eric Crichton 16clb, Geoff Dore 17tl, Graham Jennings 47bc, Nancy Sefton 23clb; **Lupe Cunha:** 37cb; **The Walt Disney Co.:** 25tc; **Mary Evans:** 28clb; **Game Boy/Battle Toads:** 43bl; **Ronald Grant Archive:** Warner Bros - *Robin Hood, Prince Of Thieves* 6cl; **Sonia Halliday:** 7tl; **Robert Harding:** 23tl; **Robert Hunt Library:** 29br; **Hutchison Library:** Julia Davey 46tr; **Image Bank:** 36tl, Ronald Johnson 17tc, Rob Atkins 23crb, Nino Mascardi endpapers, Benn Mitchell 36tl, Jurgen Vogt 19c; **Impact:** Mike McQueen 28cla; **Kobal:** 25cr; **Jaeger - LeCoultre:** 21crb; **Magnum:** Erich Hartmann 31br; **MARS/US Navy:** 28tr; **The Mews Dental Surgery:** 37cbr; **Museum of Automata, York ©:** 34cl; **National Motor Museum, Beaulieu:** 31tc; **Panos:** J. Hartley 6br; **Popperfoto:** 33tc; **Professional Sport:** 40bc; **Science Photo Library:** Alex Bartel 28bl, Professor C. Ferlaud/CNRI 37tc, Malcolm Fielding/Johnson Matthey PLC 26bl, Lowell Georgia 1c, Adam Hart-Davies 31cr, Mehau Kulyk 5bcl, 36-7c, Rory McClenaghan 37tr, Peter Menzel 32bc, Larry Mulvehill 36bl, Hank Morgan 37bl, 37cr, Philippe Plailly 23cra, St. Bartholomew's Hospital 36bc, Dr. Klaus Schiller 37tl, James Stevenson 37bc, Takeshi Takahara 9tc, Sheila Terry 34c, US Dept. of Energy 35br; **Harry Smith:** 39tc; **Snow Machines Inc.:** 40clb; **Telegraph Colour Library:** 10br; **Zefa:** 3c, 13tc, 15c, 17tr, 17bcl, 21cr, 47tl.

Every effort has been made to trace the copyright holders, and we apologize in advance for any unintentional omissions. We would be pleased to insert the appropriate acknowledgments in any subsequent edition of this publication.

t – **top**	l – **left**	a – **above**	cb – **center below**	
b – **bottom**	r – **right**	c – **center**	clb – **center left below**	crb – **center right below**

INDEX